Epic Cars

DBS Superleggera

MEGAN COOLEY PETERSON

BLACK
RABBIT
BOOKS

Bolt is published by Black Rabbit Books
P.O. Box 227, Mankato, Minnesota, 56002.
www.blackrabbitbooks.com
Copyright © 2021 Black Rabbit Books

Jen Besel, editor; Grant Gould, designer;
Omay Ayres, photo researcher

Library of Congress Cataloging-in-Publication Data
Names: Peterson, Megan Cooley, author.
Title: DBS Superleggera / by Megan Cooley Peterson.
Description: Mankato, Minnesota : Black Rabbit Books, 2021. | Series: Bolt.
  Epic cars | Includes bibliographical references and index. | Audience:
  Ages 8-12. | Audience: Grades 4-6. | Summary: "Experience what it's like
  to be behind the wheel of a DBS Superleggera through exciting text,
  vibrant photography, and labeled images and other graphics"— Provided
  by publisher.
Identifiers: LCCN 2019029055 (print) | LCCN 2019029056 (ebook) |
  ISBN 9781623102531 (hardcover) | ISBN 9781644663493 (paperback) |
  ISBN 9781623103477 (ebook)
Subjects: LCSH: DBS Superleggera automobile—Juvenile literature.
Classification: LCC TL215.A75 P48 2021 (print) | LCC TL215.A75 (ebook) |
  DDC 629.222/2—dc23
LC record available at https://lccn.loc.gov/2019029055
LC ebook record available at https://lccn.loc.gov/2019029056

BOLT

Image Credits
astonmartin-louis.com: Aston
Martin New England, 8–9; astonmartin-
washingtondc.com: Aston Martin Washing-
ton DC, 18 (t), 19 (b); autocar.co.uk: Autocar UK,
3, 19; configurator.astonmartin.com: Aston Martin,
6–7, 18 (b), 19 (t), 26 (t), 31, 32; en.wheelsage.org:
Wheelsage, 6 (t); exportwagen.eu: Exportwagen, 21; kbb.
com: Kelley Blue Book, 19 (c); media.astonmartin.com:
Aston Martin Lagonda Media, Cover (car), 4–5, 11, 12–13,
15 (t), 16–17, 18–19 (bkgd), 23 (car), 24–25, 26–27, 27
(b), 28–29 ; media.ferrari.com: Ferrari Media, 15 (b); red-
dit.com: astulz, 1; Shutterstock: Elenamiv, Cover (bkgd);
GarikProst, 23 (t)

Every effort has been made to contact
copyright holders for material reproduced in
this book. Any omissions will be rectified
in subsequent printings if notice is
given to the publisher.

Contents

CHAPTER 1

Racing

Down the Road

The Aston Martin DBS Superleggera growls down the road. This supercar combines power and **luxury**. It has the power of a race car. But its smooth body looks like a piece of art.

VANQUISH S VS. DBS SUPERLEGGERA

VANQUISH S

580
horsepower

3.5
SECONDS

TIME TO GO FROM
0 to 62 MILES
(100 KILOMETERS) PER HOUR

DBS SUPERLEGGERA

715
horsepower

The Best

Aston Martin **unveiled** the DBS Superleggera in 2018. It replaced the Vanquish. Some say the Superleggera is the best car Aston Martin has ever made. It was built for speed and for comfort.

3.4 SECONDS

TIME TO GO FROM

0 to 62 MILES

(100 KM) PER HOUR

SPOILER

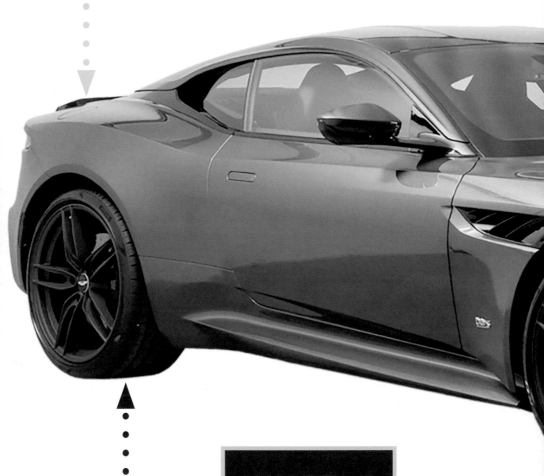

WHEELS

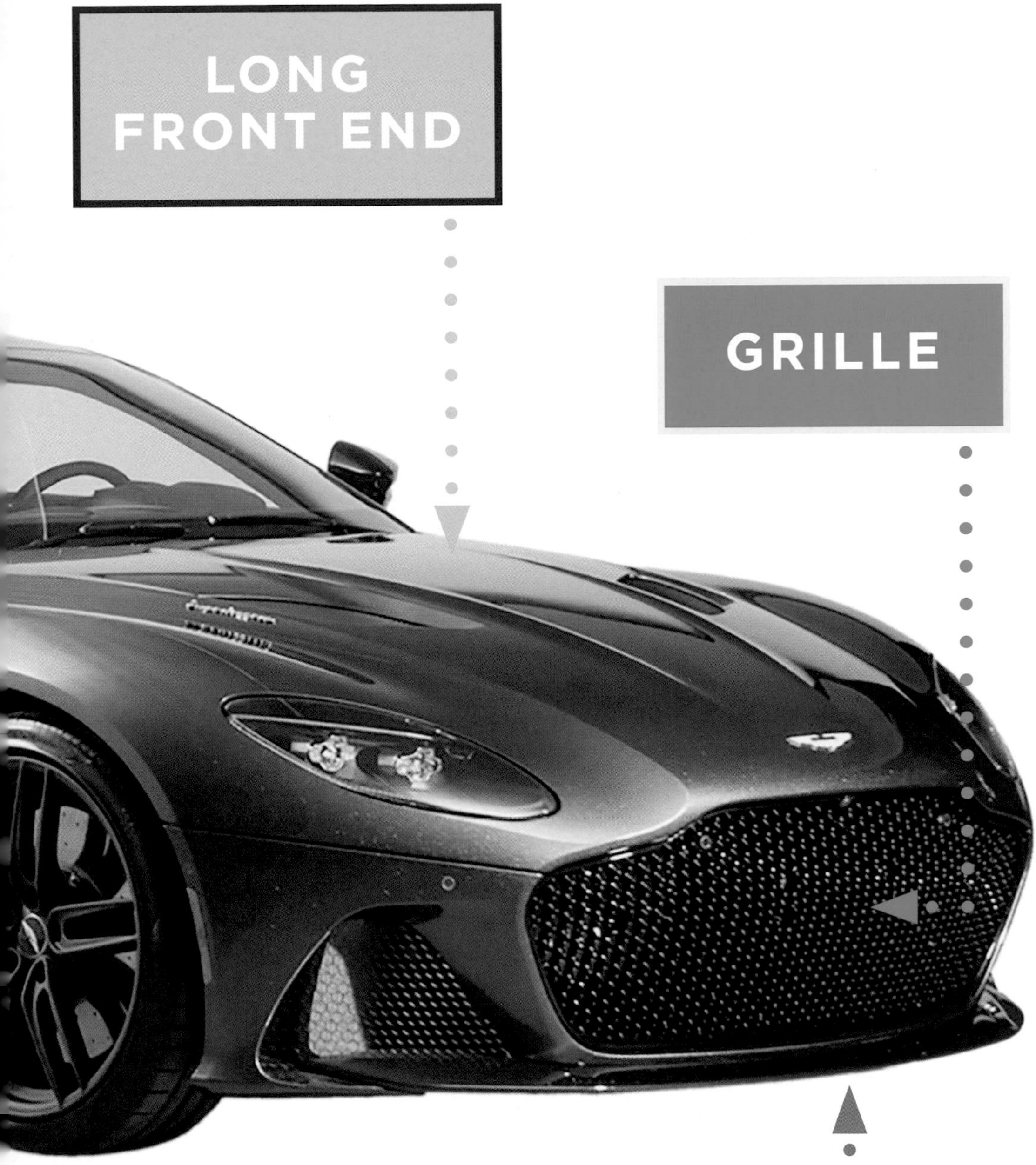

LONG
FRONT END

GRILLE

SPLITTER

9

CHAPTER 2

Design

The DBS Superleggera is a showstopper. The large black grille gives the car a mean look. The car's smooth body shape creates less **drag**. Vents at the front and back of the car create **downforce**. A splitter also keeps the car **stable** at high speeds.

More Speed

Supercar drivers want lots of speed and power. And a lighter car equals more speed. Designers gave the DBS Superleggera a lightweight aluminum frame. **Carbon fiber** body panels also keep the car light.

Each car is built by hand in Gaydon, England.

Interior

Climbing into a Superleggera is even more fun than looking at one. The car's interior has **sleek** lines and racing seats. The grille's honeycomb design is repeated in the interior. A touch screen controls the car's sound and navigation systems.

The Superleggera was built to compete with the Ferrari 812 Superfast.

Personalized

Owners can choose many of the Superleggera's options. There are dozens of interior and exterior colors to choose from. The seats come in two types of hand-stitched leather. Each Superleggera is practically one of a kind.

SMOKED OR RED TAILLIGHTS

45 PAINT COLORS

CUSTOMIZABLE
ROOF COLORS

6
WHEEL OPTIONS

5
BRAKE
CALIPER
COLORS

CHAPTER 3

Power and Performance

The Superleggera is impressive under the hood too. Its 12-cylinder, twin-turbo engine has a lot of power. This car races up to 211 miles (340 km) per hour. It's the fastest road car Aston Martin has ever made.

COMPARING TOP SPEEDS

2019 DBS Superleggera

2018 812 Superfast

2018 Porsche 911 GT3

2019 Acura NSX

miles per hour

211 (340 km)

211 (340 km)

198 (319 km)

191 (307 km)

160   170   180   190   200   210   220

Transmission

The Superleggera's **transmission** is as powerful as its engine. The eight-speed transmission sends power to the rear wheels. It also gives drivers three driving modes. Each mode gives the car different amounts of **torque**. More torque makes the car accelerate faster.

DRIVING MODES

GT

shifting is
smooth

SPORT

engine noise
gets louder

SPORT PLUS

shifting
is more
aggressive

23

Brakes

Superfast cars need super strong brakes. The Superleggera's carbon ceramic brakes stop the car in a snap. These brakes don't overheat. Overheated brakes don't work as well as cool brakes.

$304,995
BASE PRICE

185.5
INCHES
(471 CENTIMETERS)
LENGTH

By the Numbers

84.4
INCHES
(214 CM)
WIDTH

4
TOTAL SEATING

50.3
INCHES
(128 CM)
HEIGHT

CHAPTER 4

An Epic Car

The DBS Superleggera carves up the road with ease. This epic car looks like art. But it has amazing power. No wonder people say it's Aston Martin's best car.

carbon fiber (KAR-buhn FAHY-bur)—a very strong, lightweight material

downforce (doun-FAWRS)—a force that increases the stability of a motor vehicle by pressing it downward

drag (DRAYG)—something that makes action or progress slower or more difficult

luxury (LUHK-shuh-ree)—something that is expensive and not necessary

sleek (SLEEK)—straight and smooth

stable (STAY-buhl)—steady and able to resist unwanted motion

torque (TORK)—a turning or twisting force

transmission (tranz-MI-shun)—a group of parts that takes energy from the engine to an axle that moves

unveil (un-VAYL)—to make public

BOOKS

Fishman, Jon M. *Cool Sports Cars*. Awesome Rides. Minneapolis: Lerner Publications, 2019.

Garstecki, Julia. *Ferrari 812 Superfast*. Epic Cars. Mankato, MN: Black Rabbit Books, 2020.

Oachs, Emily Rose. *Aston Martin DB9*. Car Crazy. Minneapolis: Bellwether Media, Inc., 2017.

WEBSITES

2019 Aston Martin DBS Superleggera
www.caranddriver.com/reviews/a22605726/2019-aston-martin-dbs-superleggera-first-drive-review/

Aston Martin DBS Superleggera
www.astonmartin.com/en-us/models/dbs-superleggera

Aston Martin Heritage
www.astonmartin.com/en-us/our-world/heritage

INDEX